—

Player Profiles

CARLI LLOYD

KRYSTYNA PORAY GODDU

BLACK
RABBIT
BOOKS

Bolt is published by Black Rabbit Books
P.O. Box 3263, Mankato, Minnesota, 56002.
www.blackrabbitbooks.com
Copyright © 2020 Black Rabbit Books

Jennifer Besel & Marysa Storm, editors; Grant
Gould, designer; Omay Ayres, photo researcher

Names: Goddu, Krystyna Poray, author.
Title: Carli Lloyd / by Krystyna Poray Goddu.
Description: Mankato, Minnesota : Black Rabbit Books, [2020] | Series:
Bolt. Player profiles | Includes bibliographical references and index. |
Audience: Age 8-12. | Audience: Grade 4 to 6.
Identifiers: LCCN 2018047330 (print) | LCCN 2018054153 (ebook) |
ISBN 9781680728798 (e-book) | ISBN 9781680728736 (library binding) |
ISBN 9781644660768 (paperback)
Subjects: LCSH: Lloyd, Carli, 1982–Juvenile literature. | Women soccer
players–United States–Biography–Juvenile literature. | Soccer players–
United States–Biography–Juvenile literature.
Classification: LCC GV942.7.L59 (ebook) | LCC GV942.7.L59 G63 2020
(print) | DDC 796.334092 [B]-dc23
LC record available at https://lccn.loc.gov/2018047330

Printed in the United States. 2/19

Image Credits

CONTENTS

CHAPTER 1

A Talented PLAYER

The soccer ball rolls toward Carli Lloyd. She sprints to meet it and delivers a powerful kick. The ball flies toward the net. The goalkeeper dives for it. But the ball is unstoppable. Goal!

Lloyd is one of the United States' strongest soccer players. She **dominates** as a **midfielder**. She's a fast and strong kicker. Lloyd works well under pressure too. She makes incredible goals during big games.

FUN FACTS

HAS WRITTEN BOOKS ABOUT HER LIFE

CARLI LLOYD

ALL HEART
MY DEDICATION AND DETERMINATION
TO BECOME ONE OF SOCCER'S BEST

WAYNE COFFEY

CARLI LLOYD

WHEN NOBODY WAS WATCHING
My Hard-Fought Journey to the Top of the Soccer World

w/. WAYNE COFFEY

★ ★ ★ ★ ★
New York Times
BESTSELLER

"The bigger the game, the bigger the player is, when you look at it two ... be a doubt about there being a lot of mental behind it for Lloyd."
—ESPN.com

6'

5'

4'

LOVES WRITING
TO-DO LISTS

HER FAVORITE HOLIDAY IS CHRISTMAS

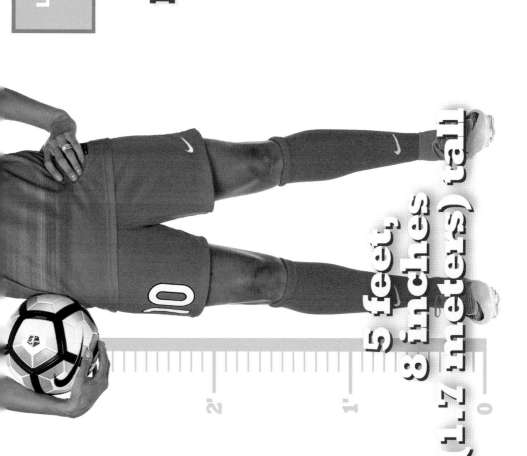

5 feet, 8 inches
(1.7 meters) tall

2'

1'

0

CHAPTER 2

Lloyd's Early  YEARS

Lloyd was born on July 16, 1982. She grew up in New Jersey. Lloyd fell in love with soccer at an early age. People often played soccer in a field near her house. She would join in the games. Sometimes nobody was playing there. So she would just practice by herself. She spent hours kicking balls.

Early Success

Lloyd was a star soccer player in high school. She also played for a local club called the Medford Strikers. With Lloyd, the Strikers won two State Cups.

After high school, Lloyd went to Rutgers University and played soccer there. During college, she also played on the **National** Under-21 Team.

In 2003, Lloyd began working with trainer James Galanis. He helped Lloyd become physically and mentally stronger. He's worked with her ever since

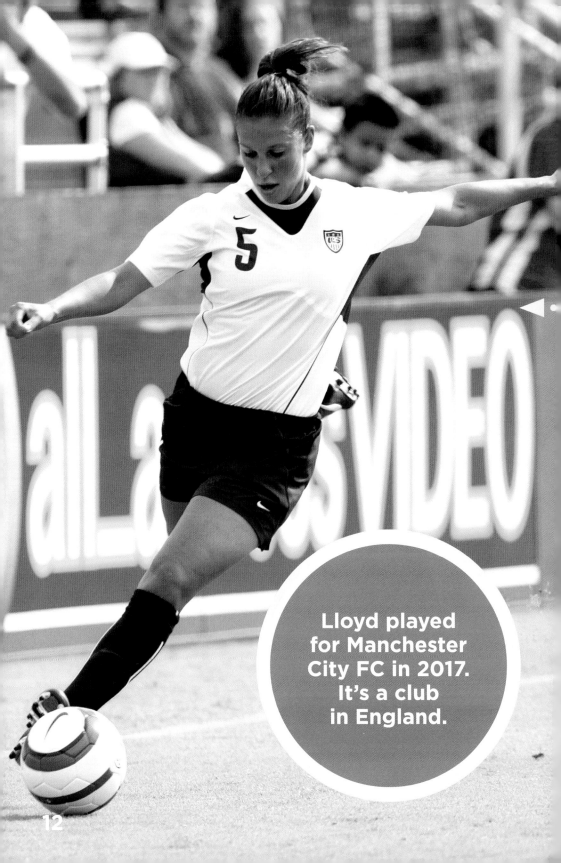

Lloyd played for Manchester City FC in 2017. It's a club in England.

CHAPTER 3

Going PRO

In 2005, Lloyd played her first game with the U.S. Women's National Team. The team, often called Team USA, plays against teams from other countries. The team competes in the Olympics and **World Cup**.

Lloyd also plays in the National Women's Soccer League. It's made up of U.S. teams that play each other. Lloyd joined the league in 2008. As of 2018, she plays for Sky Blue FC.

Going for Gold

Lloyd has gone to the 2008, 2012, and 2016 Olympics. In 2008, she scored the winning goal of the final game. Lloyd led the team to another big win in 2012. She made two goals in the final game. Team USA beat Japan 2–1.

2008	2012	2016
1st place	**1st** place	**5th** place

Winning the World Cup

In 2015, Team USA went to the World Cup. During the final match, Lloyd was unstoppable. She scored three goals in the first 16 minutes. It was the fastest **hat trick** in World Cup history. No woman had scored a hat trick in a World Cup final before. Thanks to Lloyd, Team USA won the World Cup. The team hadn't won it since 1999.

Lloyd became Team USA's co-captain in 2016.

Many Goals

In 2017, Lloyd badly **sprained** her ankle. But she didn't let the injury stop her. After only two months, Lloyd was back on the field. A few months later, she scored her 100th goal with Team USA.

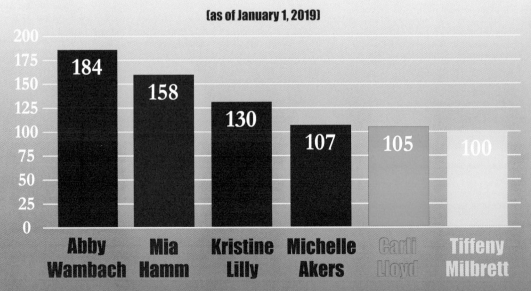

Leading Goal Scorers of the U.S. Women's National Team
(as of January 1, 2019)

Abby Wambach	Mia Hamm	Kristine Lilly	Michelle Akers	Carli Lloyd	Tiffeny Milbrett
184	158	130	107	105	100

BY THE NUMBERS

(as of 2018)

1
WORLD CUP CHAMPIONSHIP WIN

NUMBER OF OLYMPIC GOLD MEDALS

2

8 total number of Olympic goals

7 total number of World Cup goals

CHAPTER 4

On and Off the

Lloyd trains hard to do her best. She works out regularly to stay in shape. She even trains on holidays and in snow. Lloyd eats healthy too. Some of her favorite foods include salads and smoothies. She makes sure to drink a lot of water.

A Powerful Role Model

Lloyd loves soccer. She works to share the game with others. Lloyd runs soccer clinics for girls. She teaches them how to shoot and score. She helps train players from her old team, the Strikers, too.

Lloyd has also spoken out about pay **inequality**. Male soccer players make much more money than female players. Lloyd says it isn't right.

Comparing Top Players'
2018 Salaries

Lionel Messi
$84 million

Cristiano Ronaldo
$61 million

Carli Lloyd
$450,000

Alex Morgan
$450,000

Soccer Superstar

People say Lloyd is one of soccer's best players. But Lloyd still has a lot she wants to accomplish. She wants to get even better. She believes the best is yet to come.

FIFA named her Women's World Player of the Year in 2015 and 2016.

TIMELINE

1982
born in New Jersey

2008
wins gold
at Olympics

1980

2005
plays first game
with Team USA

2015
wins World Cup &
named FIFA's Women's
World Player of the Year

2018
scores 100th goal
with Team USA

2020

2012
wins gold
at Olympics

2016
named FIFA's Women's
World Player of the Year

GLOSSARY

dominate (DOM-uh-neyt)—to hold a commanding position over

FIFA—the organization that controls world soccer; FIFA is short for the International Federation of Association Football.

hat trick (HAT TRIK)—scoring three goals in one game

inequality (in-i-KWOL-i-tee)—an unfair situation in which some people have more rights or better opportunities than other people

midfielder (MID-feel-duhr)—a soccer player who plays in the middle of the field; midfielders feed the ball to the forwards.

national (NAH-shun-uhl)—relating to a country

sprain (SPREYN)—to injure by a sudden or severe twist

World Cup (WURLD KUP)—a worldwide soccer tournament held every four years; teams from around the world compete against each other.

BOOKS

Killion, Ann. *Champions of Women's Soccer.* New York: Philomel Books, 2018.

Peterson, Megan Cooley. *Stars of Women's Soccer.* On the Pitch. Mankato, MN: Black Rabbit Books, 2018.

Raum, Elizabeth. *Carli Lloyd.* Pro Sports Biographies. Mankato, MN: Amicus High Interest/ Amicus Ink, 2018.

WEBSITES

Carli Lloyd
www.ussoccer.com/players/l/carli-lloyd#tab-1

Official Website of Carli Lloyd
www.carlilloyd.com

Soccer
www.sikids.com/soccer

INDEX